Competition Law in Ecuador

Competition Law in Ecuador

Josemaría Bustamante

This book was originally published as a monograph in the International Encyclopaedia of Laws/Competition Law.

Founding Editor: Roger Blanpain
General Editor: Frank Hendrickx
Volume Editors: Francesco Denozza & Alberto Toffoletto

Wolters Kluwer

Published by:
Kluwer Law International B.V.
PO Box 316
2400 AH Alphen aan den Rijn
The Netherlands
E-mail: international-sales@wolterskluwer.com
Website: lrus.wolterskluwer.com

Sold and distributed in North, Central and South America by:
Wolters Kluwer Legal & Regulatory U.S.
7201 McKinney Circle
Frederick, MD 21704
United States of America
Email: customer.service@wolterskluwer.com

Sold and distributed in all other countries by:
Air Business Subscriptions
Rockwood House
Haywards Heath
West Sussex
RH16 3DH
United Kingdom
Email: international-customerservice@wolterskluwer.com

ISBN 978-94-035-2275-3

e-Book: ISBN 978-94-035-2280-7
web-PDF: ISBN 978-94-035-2281-4

The Author

Josemaria Bustamante has assisted international clients in Multilateral transactions; Cross Border transactions; M&A and Antitrust; Project Financing; Public Procurement; Tax Law; Commercial Law; Corporate Law; International Trade; Arbitration and Litigation in the following sectors: Insurance; Banking & Finance; Commerce; Communications and Telecommunications; Energy; Agrochemical industry; and, Food industry. Dr. Bustamante is also avid in Mediation, Arbitration, and Civil litigation. Pro bono work includes having obtained the first certificate of protection in Ecuador and the first patent conferred to a Luthier in Ecuador, which were granted to Luthier Hugo Chiliquinga; Fundación Zaldumbide-Rosales (promoting musicians worldwide); The Global Foodbanking Network, and several individuals, domestic and alien, requiring litigious assistance in Ecuador. He is a member of the Quito Bar Association and also active in the International Bar Association, the American Bar Association, the Quito Chamber of Commerce, London Chamber of Commerce, and Paris Chamber of Commerce, the Bomchil Group (an association of Latin American Law Firms), and World Services Group. He has also been a Speaker of the American and Washington State Bar Associations, the San Francisco Bar Association, the London Chamber of Commerce, and the Paris Chamber of Commerce. He is also a keen contributor to the International Encyclopedia of Laws.

Education

In 1997, Dr. Bustamante obtained a Licentiate in Juridical Sciences degree; he also obtained a Republican Courts Barrister degree and a Doctorate on Jurisprudence degree in 2004 from the Pontificia Universidad Católica del Ecuador.
Languages: Spanish and English
Born: Quito, Ecuador, September 15, 1965.

The Author

Table of Contents

General Introduction

1. In this section, statistics are based on the latest National Census conducted in 2010 by *Instituto Ecuatoriano de Estadísticas y Censos* (Ecuadorian Institute of Statistics and Census). You can access the information on the following link: http://www.ecuadorencifras.gob.ec/ (last visited 27/jan/2015)

§1. General Background of the Country

I. Geography and Weather

2. Ecuador is located in northwestern South America. It is bordered on the North by Colombia, on the South and East by Peru, and on the West by the Pacific Ocean. Ecuador is crossed by the Equator, so it benefits from being in the Northern and Southern hemisphere at a time, and by the geostationary orbit.

3. It has an area, including the Galápagos Islands, of about 283,520 km^2. The Galapagos Islands grants Ecuador the rights to a portion of the Antarctic continent.

4. Ecuador has four natural regions: Andean region, Coast region, Amazon region, and Galápagos region. Because of the variety of its geography, Ecuador has several land routes that connect the country, as well as domestic air flights. Its biggest tourist attraction is the possibility of crossing the three regions (Andean, Coast, and Amazon regions) by land in a matter of hours.

5. In the Andean region, traditional agriculture predominates with certain sectors of flower production and broccoli.

6. The Coast region is comprised essentially by industrial agriculture with cocoa and banana products par excellence. Facilities include aquaculture production due to the thoroughness of its coasts, being tuna and shrimp the main export products.

7. Instead, the Amazon region has the exploitation of natural resources, such as oil and mining, as well as having a wealth of unique flora and fauna in the World. The Galápagos region, meanwhile, is eminently touristic.

8. With four natural regions, temperatures vary from one to another and can reach below 0°C in the Andean region and up to 35°C in the Coast, Galápagos, and Amazon regions.

II. Population and Values

9. According to the latest National Census of 2010, Ecuador has 14,600,000 people. As said by estimates by the Ecuadorian Institute of Statistics and Census, the population currently exceeds 15,700,000 inhabitants, being the Coast region the most populated region.

10. The birth rate is 1.8 children, and life expectancy is 79 years on an average.

11. Due to the economic crisis experienced by the country in 1999–2000 period, about two million people emigrated, being Europe their main destination; however, in recent years, the country has seen some reception of immigrants from Colombia, Cuba, and Spain.

12. Ecuador is one of the countries having more refugees in Latin America. As of April 2013, there were 55,249 recognized refugees according to data from the Ministry of Foreign Affairs.

13. The population of Ecuador is mainly concentrated in urban areas with considerable rural migration in recent years, and this being one of the principal reasons for lack of job opportunities.

14. The country's unemployment rate is 4.57 %, and its underemployment (self-employed or partially employed) rate is higher than 42.69%. This means that people working under this system do not have all the legal rights and benefits resulting from full employment.

15. Ecuador shows constant economic and political stability since seven years ago due to a steady increase in the oil price (main export product), a better tax collection, and a change in the productive matrix from oil dependence to other sources, which has allowed unprecedented social and public investment. High-quality highways are continuously being constructed nationwide; a touristic railroad system has been renewed; more schools and hospitals have been built; the education and social security system have been renewed ensuring general public access which has, in the short term, improved the quality of life. The internal budget for the year 2013 was USD 32,366 bn; GDP for the year 2012 was USD 84,039 bn, and the external debt in relation to GDP was 13.90%.

III. Government and Politics

16. The country is organized in the form of a republic. The political system is democratic. Following the promulgation of the Constitution in 2008, the State power is divided into five Functions, adding to the classic ones, Executive Function, Judicial Function and Legislative Function, two new Functions called Participation and Social Control Function, and the Electoral Function.

17. The representatives of each of the Functions are: the President, the President of the Judicial Council, the President of the National Assembly, the President of the Council of Social Participation and Control, and the President of the National Electoral Council, respectively.

18. The territorial division of Ecuador is by provinces, each represented by its governor and provincial council. There are currently twenty-four provinces, two of them created in the past years. The Constitution recognizes these provinces as a form of self-government, so they acquired the name of "Decentralized Autonomous Governments."

§2. Economic System

19. Ecuador's Constitution (Article 283) states that the economic system is a social and solidarity system. Within this scheme, the human being is recognized as a subject and purpose. The Constitution seeks the balance between society, State and market, without neglecting the Nature, ensuring good living or *sumak kawsay* ("living well" in Kichua).

20. The recognized forms of economic organization are: public, private, mixed, popular and supportive. The latter refers to cooperative sectors, associations and community.

21. The objectives the country is aimed to reach are, among others, to promote an appropriate distribution of income and national wealth. Profile and importance are given to domestic production, so as to achieve an insertion in the world economy.

22. Food and energy security matters are essential in the current economic policy. New matrices are being developed, both productive and energy, led by the Vice-President of the Republic. These are long-term projects; therefore, it requires a continuous commitment from successive governments for their duration in time.

I. Industries and Trade

23. Ecuador is an exporter of raw materials, with oil as its main export product. It has a long tradition as an exporter of agricultural products, such as bananas and cocoa; and, in recent years, roses and vegetables. Ecuador also exports seafood. Its products are quite appreciated in the European and American markets.

24. It seeks to change the schema of being a raw materials exporter for a finished goods exporter. One of the steps to achieve this goal is the construction of the Pacific Refinery, with Venezuelan and Chinese investment, which will allow the country to refine oil for both domestic consumption and export. This project, if not deterred, is currently dormant. It seems to be a no-go, any longer. A strong investment in the agriculture sector is being made to improve the supply chain and make products more competitive in the international market.

II. Currency

25. In 2000, Ecuador adopted the U.S. dollar as the official legal tender. The exchange rate fixed at that time was ECS 25,000 per dollar. The State, due to not having its own currency, is forced to bring foreign currency through exports and remittances from migrants.

III. Taxes

26. The tax regime in Ecuador has allowed taxes to be considered as the second source of funding for the State, leaving remittances of migrants relegated, who, at the time, financed the country's economy.

27. The Internal Revenue Service is the main tax collector agent. The National Secretariat of Customs and Autonomous Governments (Municipalities, Provincial Councils and others) are also collector agents, according to their capability in specific jurisdictions.

§3. Legal System

28. Article 1 of our current Constitution states that "Ecuador is a constitutional State of rights and justice, social, democratic, sovereign, independent, unitary, intercultural, plurinational and secular. It is organized as a republic and governed in a decentralized manner. Sovereignty resides in the people, whose will is the foundation of authority, and is exercised through public bodies and forms of direct participation under the Constitution. Non-renewable natural resources of the territory of the State belong to their birthright, inalienable, imprescriptible patrimony."

29. The legal system is based on two instances, judges and provincial courts. There is the National Court before which only cassations are processed, and therefore, it is not considered as a third instance. Furthermore, the Constitutional Court is only capable of processing constitutional actions; so, it is not considered as a process instance.

§4. HISTORICAL BACKGROUND OF ANTITRUST LAW

30. As a result of the promulgation of the Constitution in 1998, interest for treating the subject to rule free competition within the Ecuadorian legal system resurged. Some attempts were given for enacting an Antitrust Act seeking to protect, in the first place, the consumers' right, as well as the sustainability of the enterprises in the market.

31. The State Modernization Act of 1993 was the first statute to mention the prohibition of monopolies (Article 47). This Act, abrogated by Administrative Code of 2017, authorized third parties the establishment of activities or the rendering of services of equal or similar nature as a way to prevent monopoly. Expressly stating that in the case of concessions, licenses or permits, they may be granted on exclusive regulated conditions, only for a specified period, with the authorization of the President of the Republic by Executive Decree, or the competent body in the case of sectional governments.

32. Likewise, the amendment of August 2000, mentioned that when the award of a public service involves a dominant market position, its titleholder cannot be the owner, neither by himself nor by third parties, of mass media or financial institutions. Each of these activities should be developed exclusively by its administrators or owners.

33. Framed in the new constitutional order of the Constitution of 2008, which clearly states that the State will regulate, monitor and intervene, when necessary, in trade and economic transactions; and will punish exploitation, usury, hoarding, simulation, speculative trading of goods and services, as well as all forms of damages to economic rights and public and collective goods (Article 335). It also mentions that the State will define a price policy oriented to protect domestic production, will establish sanction mechanisms to avoid any practice of private monopoly and oligopoly, or abuse of dominant position in the market, and other unfair competitive practices (Article 335).

34. On the basis of the provisions in Article 336, this expressly sets forth that the State will promote and ensure fair trade as a means of access to quality goods and services, minimizing distortions of intermediation and promoting sustainability. The State will ensure transparency and efficiency in the markets and will promote competition in equal opportunities and conditions, which will be defined by the law.

35. The process of drafting the Regulation and Market Power Control Organic Act began in August 2011, until its enactment in October of that year. This occurred because the Act was presented by the President as a matter of "economic emergency," which expedited the process for publishing the law.

Part I. Structure of Antitrust Law and Its Enforcement

Chapter 1. Sources of Antitrust Law

§1. National Sources

36. As supreme law in the first place is the Constitution. Below the Constitution are the duly enacted International Treaties, and then the Antitrust Act.

37. The Constitution sets forth in Article 52 the right people have to dispose of goods and services of optimal quality, based on accurate and not misleading information on its content and characteristics.

38. It is also set forth that the State shall promote the fair and complementary trade of goods and services in transparent and efficient markets (Article 284).

39. It seeks to give greater importance to the development, strengthening and encouragement of the domestic market based on the National Development Plan. It expressly prohibits monopolies and oligopolies, which affect the proper functioning of markets (Article 304).

40. In that sense, it provides for the power of the State to regulate, control and intervene, when necessary, in the market's economic trade and transactions. Especially, through a pricing policy that is aimed to protecting domestic production, punishing any practice of private monopoly and oligopoly, or abuse of dominant position in the market and other unfair competitive practices (Article 335).

§2. International Sources

41. Decision 608 of the Andean Community of Nations was issued in 2005. This Andean provision is mainly related to rules for the protection and promotion of free competition. In 2009, the current Government issued Decree 1614, which established the procedure for the application of the Community rule.

§3. SECONDARY SOURCES

I. Regulations

42. Regulations to be passed by the Board of Regulation of Market Power.

43. Regulation For The Operation Of The Board of Regulating of the Regulation and Control of Market Power Organic Law and Its Permanent Secretariat.- It rules the operation of the Regulatory Board of the Organic Law for the Regulation and Control of Market Power, hereinafter "Regulatory Board and its Permanent Secretariat."

44. Threshold on the Amount of Total Business Turnover in Ecuador, the Aggregate Of Stakeholders in an Economic Concentration Operation which Must Comply with Prior Notification Procedure.- It sets forth the thresholds on the amount of total turnover in Ecuador of all stakeholders of an economic concentration operation, on which it must necessarily be notified to the Superintendency in accordance with the provisions of paragraph (a) of Article 16 of the Law.

45. Regulations issued by the Superintendency of Control of Market Power

46. Currently, there are the following regulations:

47. Experts Accreditation Regulation: It sets forth the rules governing for all professionals and technicians who have academic or technical expertise; and proven, sufficient and necessary experience to intervene as experts in administrative procedures that are substantiated in the Superintendency.

48. Rate for Analysis and Study of Concentration Operations Subject to Mandatory Notification: Economic operators complying with the provisions of Article 16 of the Regulation and Control of Market Power Organic Law are required to pay a fee to the Superintendency of Control of Market Power for analysis and study of mergers subject to mandatory notification.

49. Form for Notification of Economic Concentration Operations: The notification form for mandatory or informative concentration operations is required to be submitted to the Superintendency of Control of Market Power by economic operators engaged in economic concentrations operations

II. Guidelines

50. These are the following guidelines up to this date:

Instructive document on Substantiation of Research Procedures in Administrative Office. It is aimed to determine the actions in procedures for market research and the substantiation of researches and penalties, in order to operationalize the procedure set forth in the Law and Regulations which will correspond to the scope of application of investigative bodies.

51. Manual for Procedures for Application of Commitments of Cessation.- The main purpose of the Commitments of Cessation is to adjust the behavior of operators under the Law, without substantiating the whole process and come to penalties provided for in Article 79 of Regulation and Control of Market Power Organic Act. Through the implementation of commitments of cease, it is aimed to minimize further the expenditure of the State's resources generated in the research process.

52. Special Instructive Document for the Conduct of Searches and Inspections Within the Power to Research; and for Regulation of the Chain of Custody.- The purpose of this Instructive Document is to establish minimum procedural rules to be observed during inspections and searches within the administrative procedures performed by the Superintendency of Control of Market Power, to obtain objects, elements, information, documents, or instruments, which are gathered in the place that was searched or inspected; and, once obtained, to keep them in perfect condition, and maintain the proper conservation throughout the investigation procedure which will contribute to clarify the possible behaviors contrary to the law.

53. Special Instructive Document for Application of Precautionary Measures.- The purpose of this Instructive Document is to set forth the procedure for adoption of precautionary measures in Administrative Office to prevent highly detrimental effects on the market until the Resolution of the Resolution Commission of First Instance; as well as to ensure the effectiveness of the final Resolution; observing the principles of non-discrimination, transparency, proportionality, and due process.

54. Instructive Document for Procedural Management of Files and their Replacement in Case of Loss or Destruction.- The purpose of this Instructive Document is to set forth treatment that the Superintendency of Control of Market Powers' Bodies must necessarily observe in the management of Files generated within the competence of the institution. This Instructive Document is mandatory for internal administrative level, that is, the different agencies which have substantiation of administrative proceedings under their responsibility.

§4. Sources' Relation and Hierarchy

55. Article 425 of the Constitution sets forth the hierarchical order of application of the rules that basic Kelsenian model is structured as follows: The Constitution; international treaties; organic congress acts; ordinary congress acts; regional rules and district ordinances; decrees and regulations; ordinances; agreements and resolutions; and other acts and decisions of public authorities.

56. Only Justices of the Constitutional Court have jurisdiction for interpreting Constitutional provisions. However, former Constitutions established that any rule (including Regulations), although illegal or unconstitutional, was applicable and considered licit unless and until duly voided through due process. Only judges were allowed to apply the highest hierarchical rule. Current Constitution provides that any public officer is bound to apply the highest hierarchical rule.

§5. Role and Authority of Precedents

57. Competition Act does not set forth the obligation to take into account the precedents as a source of rules; however, they are used as a reference source for both economic operators and for the control body. On the other hand, three rulings by the National Court on the same matter are considered to be compulsory precedents. The National Court is also empowered to issue compulsory interpretations.

Chapter 2. Scope of Application

§1. Territorial Reach

58. This Act applies to those economic activities involving economic operators (understanding economic operators as domestic and foreign persons, moral persons or legal persons, public or private), to be developed within the country and outside, to the extent that the events will occur, or may have harmful effects on the domestic market.

§2. Special Sectors

59. According to our Constitution (Article 313), *the State reserves the right to administer, regulate, control and manage strategic sectors* based on the principles of environmental sustainability, precaution, prevention, and efficiency.

60. Strategic sectors are understood as *those whose importance and magnitude have vital economic, social, political or environmental influence*, such as: energy in all its forms, telecommunications, non-renewable natural resources, transportation and refining hydrocarbons, biodiversity and genetic patrimony, radio-electrical spectrum, water, and others determined by law.

Energy Sector

61. One of the main columns of our economy is the sector of energy, especially oil. It is the first generator of revenue after taxes. That is the reason for the importance of this sector for the economic development of the country.

62. Pursuant to the Ministry Coordinator of Strategic Sectors, our current Energy Matrix is dependent on more than 50% in the energy generated by fuel combustion,[1] followed by hydropower generation. There are currently thirty-three Hydroelectric plants, and eight more are under construction, and far behind the energy generated by renewable energy. Hence, the change of the energy matrix has been raised as a State policy for the coming years to reduce fuel use and increase the use of renewable energy.

63. Currently, there are several new power generation projects based on renewable energy, mainly solar and wind energy, although there are talks about geothermal and biomass generation. Wind farms are already in operation in *Galápagos* and *Bolivar* Provinces with sufficient generation capacity for self-consumption. All this is a part of the change in the Energy Matrix, which aims to have a maximum of 6% of power generation based on renewable energy.

1. http://www.sectoresestrategicos.gob.ec/, Ministry Coordinator of Strategic Sectors

64. In addition, all the public illumination is being changed to energy saving led-bulbs.

The State is allowed to grant concessions to the private sectors for power generation, but only the State is entitled to provide transmission and distribution. Hence, the talk of a State monopoly in the electricity sector, since the participation of private economic operators is only exceptionally in the generation process.

Telecommunications Sector

65. The first regulation passed by the Market Power Control Superintendence was in this sector of the economy.

66. On April 30, 2013, the Commission for Resolution of First Instance of the Superintendence of Market Power Control issued a preventive measures order based on Article 65 of the Act. The order followed a complaint filed by a State body against a private economic operator for the alleged abuse of market power. The alleged abuse consisted of drafting exclusivity clauses in lease agreements entered into with the owners of the real estate properties, in which the private economic operator maintains its infrastructure, preventing the use of these lands to other competitors.

67. The Intendancy of Investigation of Abuse of Market Power, Restrictive Agreements and Practices issued a suggestion report on Precautionary Measures. It mentions that *"it is derived from the limitation on the users to greater offer and diversification of supply and telecommunications goods and services. In this sense, provided the economic operator were infringing numbers 1, 7, 10 and 19 of Article 9 of the Act, through the imposition of the exclusivity clause."*

68. Therefore, the Commission ordered as a precautionary measure to provisionally suspend exclusivity clauses contained in the lease agreements signed by the economic operators to lease buildings for installation of radio bases and complementary infrastructure. Thus, contractual conditions are regulated to avoid market rigidity.

69. This economy's sector is one of the most concentrated sectors existing in Ecuador, as there are only three economic operators: two private ones and one of the State. It is a country where there are more telephone lines than people, so it is important to consider the market power that these economic operators have because it is practically monopolized by private companies, while the State owns only 1% of the market.

Pharmaceutical Sector

70. As per a seminar lectured by Antitrust Superintendence, of May 16, and 17, 2013[2], the drug market is one of the sectors where abuses of power and collusive practices are more common. This problem, of which Ecuador is no exception, occurs in most countries around the world when multinationals significantly increase their presence in the market.

71. Many of these market distortions, such as surcharge, poor quality and lack of access, could be corrected with proper regulation and State control. However, we must not fall into the stigma that pharmaceuticals are bad per se; the market conditions are unequal, which allow them to abuse.

72. We could not have medicines for common diseases without them, worse for catastrophic or terminal diseases. The question is—how much money is enough to make the business attractive? Without an interesting rate of return on investment or a significant profit, would the drug market be as good to invest in?

73. Ecuador believes that by generating competition from the State, these business malpractices may cease. Thus, the drug public company *ENFARMA EP* was created in December 2009. Since then, it has had little prominence in the market, being a company that has not been able to cope with large multinationals.

74. However, this market bases its structure on legal restrictions, such as patents which are granted by the State itself. These legal monopolies should not be considered as a concentration of market power. This legal restriction confers a benefit to the titleholder for a specific time that, when it expires, any other company may produce the same goods, resulting in new market competition.

75. The problem arises with the actions or omissions made during the term of such legal protection. Hence, it is imperative for the State to monitor, regulate, control and sanction any act that adversely affects the market.

76. In this sense, the Superintendency is drafting a Manual of Good Business Practices for Pharmaceutical Establishments, which shall be aimed at establishing fair trading of drugs in Ecuador.

77. Parameters regulating contractual relationships of pharmaceutical establishments are also set forth in this Manual, trying to avoid agreements and restrictive practices. That is why pharmaceutical establishments shall only be able to perform certain activities set forth expressly and specifically by the Superintendency of Control of Market Power.

---

2. http://www.scpm.gob.ec/descargas-9no-seminario-internacional-iv-de-tecnologia-y-regulacion-mercado-de-farmacos-en-el-ecuador/

Financial Sector

78. One of the sectors which experienced more changes in recent times is the financial sector. Since the amendment approved in the referendum and popular consultation of May 7, 2011, in which the directors and main shareholders could no longer be holders, directly or indirectly, of shares and participations in companies outside the financial activity or communication. Likewise, it was prohibited for entities or financial groups, their legal representatives, members of the board of directors and shareholders to participate in the control over capital, investment, or equity of social media.

79. As the enactment of the Redistribution of Income for Social Spending Organic Act in late 2012, in which the profits of these were intended to increase the *Bono de Desarrollo Humano* (Human Development Bond), financial institutions (FIs) have had to modify their business plans to adapt to constant changes in the rules.

80. In early 2013, Banco Territorial of the city of Guayaquil was closed for alleged illiquidity caused by a lack of fresh capital allowing to maintain the bank's operations. This added to a number of irregularities and caused the closing of the oldest bank in Ecuador.

81. The financial system has been accused, on more than one occasion, that there are too many financial institutions for such a small market. Therefore, the matter of adjustments aims for a reorganization of the financial system.

82. Pursuant to a media publication, this State vision makes sense if we begin to see how the financial system is nowadays. Among the 25 largest business groups in the country, there are four banks handling between 60% and 80% of the most relevant financial aggregates which are: deposits, equity, assets and income amount.[3] Hence, many sectors are of the opinion that these four financial institutions impose credit conditions.

Media Sector

83. The new Communication Organic Act was published in the Official Gazette on June 25, 2013. This Act creates a turning point in the way that the media sector was being handled in the country.

84. New distribution parameters of the frequencies in the spectrum were established: 34% for community media, 33% for public media, and the remaining 33% for for-profit private businesses.

3. http://www.telegrafo.com.ec/economia/item/11-nuevos-grupos-inyectan-mas-recursos-al-fisco.html

85. Likewise, minimum standards will be set forth for media contents, having a mandatory minimum of 50% of national production to be transmitted in the radio spots; and, 40% of national production in audiovisual space.

86. Competition is limited, with the restriction that local media may not belong in whole or in part, directly or indirectly, to foreign organizations or companies domiciled outside the Ecuadorian State, nor to foreign citizens. This is in general terms with the exceptions established by law.

87. Similarly, competition is affected by the fact that the Law provides that advertising must be produced by Ecuadorian individuals and moral persons; in the latter case, the performance and production must be made at least by 80% of Ecuadorian citizens or foreigners living in the country. This point applies to all economic operators equally; however, due to the irrelevant size of these economic operators; virtually everyone at some point uses advertising.

88. So far, only the telecommunications sector has been intervened by the Superintendence, which ordered that Exclusivity Clauses in the lease agreements for repeater antennas nationwide be removed, thus promoting any cell phone company to be able to use these antennas to improve their service coverage, and then to improve the service provided to the end user.

89. By a legal provision contained in the Communications Act, the distribution of frequencies of radio spectrum, intended for operation of Free-to-air (FTA) radio and television stations shall be distributed equally into three parts, reserving 33% of these frequencies for the operation of public media; 33% for the operation of private media; and, 34% for the operation of community media (Article 106, Communications Act).

90. In the same sense, the Communications Act prohibits natural persons or legal persons from concentrating or accumulating frequencies, concessions or signals for operating matrix radio and television stations. It prohibits the telecommunications authority from awarding more than one frequency concession for AM matrix radio, a frequency for FM radio, and a frequency for television matrix to the same natural person or legal person throughout the national territory. (Article 113, Communication Law)

Commercial Sector

91. In the past, the Superintendent of Control of Market Power was interested in regulating relationships in the commercial sector. Therefore, the Manual of Good Business Practices for the Supermarket Industry and/or similar and their Suppliers was published on December 30, 2014. This manual regulates operators conducting their commercial intermediation activities in all or in part of the Ecuadorian territory, and, for all supermarkets suppliers and/or similar who are engaged or shall be engaged in contractual commerce relationships of intermediation in the sector of food and non-food goods for daily consumption.

92. Also, the Manual of Good Business Practices for Sales and/or Marketing Sector through Independent Autonomous Sellers is being drafted, which is aimed to regulate the sales and/or the marketing sector. It does not define what is meant by the independent, autonomous seller; however, persons such as those performing catalog sales or commission agents could well enter this group.

§3. State-Owned Enterprises and Public Utilities

93. The law makes no distinction between the private sector and government entities when being subjected to regulations established by the law.

§4. Sensible Effect and *De Minimis*

94. The law states that the prohibitions in Article 11 (prohibited agreements and practices) will not be applied to those conducts of economic operators that due to its small scale operation and, therefore, its low impact in the market, are not able to significantly affect competition.

95. By resolution 003, the Regulatory Board set forth the "Criteria for Applying *De Minimis* Rule in Matter of Antitrust." It determines that prohibitions contained in Article 11 of the Act shall not apply when:

- Behaviors between actual or potential competition economic operators: when the combined market share of the parties to the agreement does not exceed 14% in any of the affected relevant markets.
- Behaviors between non-competition economic operators, not actual or potential: when the market share of each of the participants does not exceed 15% in any of the affected relevant markets.
- When, in a relevant market, competition is restricted by the cumulative effects of parallel agreements for the sale of goods or services concluded by different suppliers or distributors, the percentage of market share specified in the preceding paragraphs shall be reduced to 5%. It is understood that there is a cumulative effect if at least 30% of the reference market is covered by parallel agreement networks.

96. These criteria should be reviewed on an annual basis, or ex officio by the Regulatory Board.

97. There is no information on cases that have been based on this provision yet.

Chapter 3. Overview of Substantive Provisions

§1. Restrictive Agreements

98. Article 11 of the law sets forth that the acts performed or behavior showed by two or more economic operators, regardless of how they are expressed, regarding the production and exchange of goods or services, purporting to carry out, may carry out or cause the prevention, restriction, falsification or distortion of competition, or adversely affect economic efficiency or general welfare.

99. The law does not set forth a specific definition of "agreement" since it uses several terms that can determine the act or conduct of restricting competition.

100. In particular, the following behaviors are considered prohibited agreements and practices:

(1) To fix on a concerted basis, or manipulate the prices, interest rates, fees, discounts, or other business or transaction conditions, or exchange information with the same object or effect.
(2) To distribute, restrict, limit, paralyze, establish obligations or control, on a concerted basis, the production, distribution or marketing of goods or services.
(3) Concerted distribution of customers, suppliers or geographical areas.
(4) To distribute or restrict supply sources.
(5) To restrict technological development or investment.
(6) Acts or omissions to act, concerted agreements or practices, and generally all demeanor or bearing of providers or suppliers, whatever form they take, purported to prevent, restrict, falsify or distort the competition, either in the submission of tenders and biddings, or by seeking to secure the result in its personal gains or other supplier's or bidder's gain in a tender, competition, auctions, public auctions, or any other, as set forth in the rules governing public procurement, or in private contracting processes open to the public.
(7) Unreasonable dumping in trade, or unreasonable terms and conditions on trading goods or services.
(8) Concerted implementation, in business or service relationships of dissimilar conditions, to equivalent transactions, which unjustifiably place some competitors at a disadvantage as compared to others.
(9) To concert in order to deter an economic operator from a particular behavior, retaliating or forcing him to act in a certain manner.
(10) Agreeing to the quality of the products when they do not correspond to national or international standards.
(11) Agreeing to the subordination of execution of contracts subject to the acceptance of supplementary obligations which, by their nature or according to commercial usage, have no connection with the matter of such contracts.
(12) Unreasonable conditioned and tied sale.

(13) To refuse, on a concerted and unjustified basis, to meet the demands of purchase or acquisition, or offers for sale and provision of goods or services, or to negotiate with current or potential suppliers, distributors, dealers, purchasers or users.
(14) To unreasonably deny the admission of economic operators to an association, union or a similar entity.
(15) Boycott aimed at limiting market access, or the exercise of jurisdiction by other companies.
(16) To suspend, on a concerted and vertical basis, the provision of a monopoly service in the market to a supplier of public or private goods or services.
(17) Concerted and unreasonable fixing of resale prices.
(18) Raising entry and/or exit barriers in a relevant market.
(19) To establish, impose or suggest exclusive distribution or sale contracts, non-competition clauses or similar, being unreasonable.
(20) Those behaviors that prevent or hinder access or permanence of actual or potential competitors in the market for reasons other than economic efficiency.
(21) Agreements between suppliers and buyers, regardless of the provisions of the law, which may occur in public procurement, focusing and concentrating procurement, in an effort to favor one or more economic operators unfairly.

Agreements, practices, decisions, and recommendations which, being prohibited under the provisions of this Article, are not protected by the exemptions set for in this law, are void.

§2. Dominant Undertakings

101. Article 9 of the Act details conducts which comprise abuse of market power.

1.- Conducts of one or more economic operators to enable them to affect, actually or potentially, the participation of other competitors and the ability of entry or expansion of the latter in a relevant market, through any means outside their own competitiveness or efficiency;
2.- Conducts of one or more economic operators with market power, allowing them to increase their profit margins by extracting unjustified consumer surplus. The intention here is correct. The consumer should not pay too much for a product that is not worth it;
3.- Conducts of one or more economic operators with market power, in conditions in which due to the concentration of the means of production or marketing, such conducts affect or may affect, limit or prevent the participation of competitors or harm the direct producers, consumers and/or users;
4.- Predatory or exploitative pricing;
5.- Unjustified alteration of production levels, market or technical or technological development that adversely affect economic operators or consumers. This point might be favorable for the market in general. It must be

promoted that economic operators always seek efficiency and effectiveness, and to prevent that the market is affected for their negligence.;

6.- Unjustified price discrimination, conditions or pricing procedures;

7.- The application, in trade or service relationships, of dissimilar conditions to equivalent benefits, unreasonably puts some competitors at a disadvantage as compared to others;

8.- Conditional selling and tied selling, not justified;

9.- Unjustified refusal to meet demands for the purchase or acquisition, or acceptance of offers for the sale or supply of goods or services;

10.- The incitement, persuasion or coercion of third parties to refuse, limit or prevent the purchase, sale, mobilization or delivery of goods or the rendering of services to others;

11.- Fixing taxation limit or unjustified establishment of conditions for the exclusive purchase, sale and distribution of goods or services;

12.- Unjustified establishment of cross subsidies, particularly aggravated when these subsidies are regressive in nature;

13.- Subordination of acts, agreements or contracts subject to acceptance of obligations, fringe benefits, or conditioned that, by their nature or according to commercial usage, have no connection with the subject matter hereof;

14.- The unjustified refusal of access of other economic operators to networks or other infrastructure in return for reasonable remuneration, provided that such networks or infrastructure constitute an essential facility;

15.- The implementation of exclusionary practices or exploitative practices;

16.- The conditional discounts, such as those conferred through the sale of membership cards, loyalty or other types of constraints, involving any payment to access the above discounts;

17.- The abuse of intellectual property rights, according to the provisions of international instruments, conventions and treaties concluded and ratified by Ecuador and the law governing the matter;

18.- Unjustified implementation of a legal action that results in the restriction of access or permanence of current or potential competitors in the market;

19.- To establish, impose or suggest exclusive distribution or sale contracts, non-competition clauses or similar, that are unjustified;

20.- Unjustified resale pricing;

21.- To hold the purchase or sale to the condition of not using, buying, selling or supplying produced goods or services, processed, distributed or marketed by a third party;

22.- Those conducts that prevent or hinder access to or permanence of current or potential competitors in the market for reasons other than economic efficiency;

23.- The imposition of unreasonable conditions to suppliers or buyers, such as the setting of excessive and unjustified payment deadlines, product returns, especially when they be perishable, or requiring additional contributions or benefits of any kind which are not related to the main provision, or related to the effective provision of a service provider.

102. Undoubtedly, one of the main questions that the Act reflects is the subjective criteria. The potentiality, by not being something concrete and specific, could allow, in practice, that its true conception be oversized.

§3. Concentrations

103. The issue of economic concentration (Article 14) may generate conflicts in the future when the Superintendency starts with relevant administrative processes. The Regulator may order disinvestments, division or spin-offs in cases where it determines that that is the only way to restore competition (Article 79); likewise, it may prevent the merging of two companies with market power, in order to avoid affecting the rest of the competition.

104. Therefore, companies wishing to merge must be authorized by the Superintendency of Market Power Control to do so, which, in practice, could become one of the most difficult filters to overcome besides, increasing costs due to the fees to be paid for "analysis and study," according to Resolution No.002 of the Superintendency.

105. In turn, as a form of control, especially for large economic operators, the Act in Article 16 sets forth the obligation of Prior Notice. The Regulation defines two types of notices, mandatory notice and informative notice. A mandatory notice is applicable when the total turnover in Ecuador of all participants exceed, in the financial year preceding the operation, the amount established by the Board of Regulation. The informative notice is applicable in, concentrations involving economic operators engaged in the same activity, and, as a result of the concentration, a share of less than 30% of the relevant market for the product or service at the national level, or in a market defined within the same geographical is acquired or increased.

106. The problem is that in the absence of technical rules, which must be enacted by the Board of Regulation, there are no parameters to determine which operators are required to submit the information to the Superintendence, so that, in practice, the control body has currently received seventy-seven proceedings, twenty-six of which have been resolved, and fifty-one are pending[4]. Huge amounts of unnecessary requests for notification of economic concentration result in a high and meaningless wastage of resources.

§4. Other Prohibitions

107. The law also sets forth in Article 10 the prohibition of exploitation, by one or more economic operators, of the situation of economic dependence in which their

4. http://www.scpm.gob.ec/wp-content/uploads/2013/09/Casos-de-SPCM2.pdf

clients or suppliers may be, which do not have an equivalent alternative to exercise their activity. This behavior is considered in the following cases:

(1) Termination, even partially, of an established business relationship without any written prior notice, required with a minimum of thirty days in advance unless it is due to serious breaches by the supplier or purchaser on the conditions agreed, or in cases of force majeure.
(2) To obtain or attempt to obtain, under the threat of breaking of a business relationship or any other threat, prices, payment terms, and terms of sale, payment of additional charges and other terms of trade cooperation not included in the general conditions of sale which have been agreed upon.
(3) Use of market power to generate or maintain the position of economic dependence of one or more operators aimed at obtaining additional advantages which are not granted or would be granted to similar buyers or suppliers.
(4) Imposition, directly or indirectly, of prices or other unfair trading or services conditions.

108. Public entities responsible for the regulation of production in each of the productive sectors shall monitor the strict observance of this prohibition, especially in exchanges of small and medium food producers and popular and solidarity economy with intermediary networks of the private sector; and in case breaches are identified, it shall take appropriate measures within its competence, including an obligation to inform the Superintendent of Control of Market Power for research and respective sanction.

§5. Tests of Illegality

I. Per Se Prohibitions and Naked Restraints

109. N/A

II. Balancing Tests

110. N/A

III. Merger Tests

111. As a way of control, especially for large economic operators, the law in Article 16 establishes the obligation of Prior Notice. The regulation defines two types of notices, the compulsory notice and the voluntary notice. A compulsory notice is applicable when the total turnover in Ecuador of all participants exceed, in the financial year preceding the operation, the amount established by the Board of Regulation. The voluntary notice is applicable in, concentrations involving economic operators engaged in the same activity, and, as a result of the concentration, a share of less than 30% of the relevant market for the product or service at the national level, or in a market defined within the same geographical is acquired or increased.

Chapter 4. Overview of Main Notions

§1. Undertaking

112. The concept of an economic operator is quite broad, as it covers individuals or moral persons, public or private, domestic and foreign, whether they are for-profit or non-for-profit.

113. In addition, it states that economic operators are the ones currently or potentially performing economic activities in the country or outside the country and that their effects affect the domestic market.

114. Unions, groups, joint ventures and all forms of lawful organizations are also considered as economic operators.

115. The Regulation to the Act sets forth that the group of companies or economic operators whose turnover should be added according to the provisions contained in the law belong to an economic group.

116. However, the Regulatory Board may issue parameters which may consider other factors of the relationship between the parties that make economic groups.

117. For cases of acquisition of a portion of one or more economic operators in the same economic group, and regardless that such a party has own legal personality, it should only be taken into account, with respect to the acquired party, the turnover for the part to be acquired; i.e., the total turnover of a participant company will not consider the resulting turnover of transactions that took place between companies in the same economic group.

§2. Relevant Market

118. Relevant market takes into account geographical factors, particular characteristics of buyers and sellers participating in this market, as well as the market for the product or service.

119. The geographic market comprises the place where alternative sources of supply of the relevant product are located. This requires evaluating transportation costs, terms of sale, and existing trade barriers.

120. Competitors in a relevant market must be equivalent, for which characteristics of the sales area, the set of goods offered, the type of intermediation and differentiation with other distribution channels, should be considered.

121. The market for the product or service includes, at least, the goods or service matter of the investigated conduct and their substitutes. The Regulator is required to evaluate the preferences of customers or consumers; the characteristics, uses and prices of potential substitutes; replacement costs, as well as technological possibilities and the time required for the replacement.

§3. Market Power/Dominant Position

122. The concept of market power enshrined in the Act is the ability of economic operators to significantly influence the market, where, by any means, be able to act independently regardless of their competitors, buyers, customers, suppliers, consumers, users, distributors or other subjects participating in the market.

123. The Act makes it clear that having market power by itself is not banned. The banning is if by using that power, competition is prevented, restricted, falsified or distorted, and economic efficiency or general welfare or the rights of consumers or users is harmed (Article 7).

§4. Agreements and Concerted Practices

124. These acts and demeanors are:

- An agreement to fix or manipulate prices, interest rates or fees.
- An agreement to control the production, distribution or marketing of goods or services.
- An agreement to divide the market by customers, suppliers or geographical areas.
- An agreement to share clients, purveyors or geographical zones.
- An agreement to distribute or restrict supply sources.
- An agreement to restrict technological development or investments.
- Conducts whose purpose or effect is the prevention, restriction, falsification or distortion of competition in a public tender or private procurement processes open to the public.
- Unjustifiably discriminative prices, conditions or negotiation modalities of goods or services.
- The concerted application, in trade or service relationships, of dissimilar conditions to equivalent transactions that unreasonably put some competitors at a disadvantage as compared to others.
- To agree in order to dissuade an economic operator in certain conduct, apply reprisals or force him to act in a certain way.
- To manipulate the quality of the products, in detriment of the corresponding technical standards.
- To arrange the subordination of the entering into of contracts subject to acceptance of additional services that, by their nature or according to commercial usage, have no connection with the subject of such contracts.
- The conditional selling and tied selling that is unjustified.

- To refuse in concert and to unreasonably meet the demands of purchase or acquisition or offers of sale and rendering of products or services, or to negotiate with current or potential suppliers, distributors, dealers, purchasers or users.
- To unreasonably deny the admission of economic operators to an association, union, or similar body.
- The boycott aimed to limit market access or the exercise of competition by other companies.
- To suspend in concert and vertically, the provision of a monopoly service in the market for a supplier of goods or services, public or private.
- Concerted and unjustified resale pricing.
- To raise barriers of entry and/or exit in a relevant market.
- To establish, impose or suggest exclusive distribution or sale contracts, non-competition clauses or similar, that are unjustified.
- Those behaviors that prevent or hinder access to or permanence of current or potential competitors in the market for reasons other than economic efficiency;
- Agreements between suppliers and buyers, in an effort to favor one or more economic operators unfairly.

125. The law considers both the agreements and decisions of companies and actions that prevent, restrict, falsify or distort competition, and thus adversely affect the general welfare.

126. Vertical agreements have no special treatment. They are considered restrictive agreements and practices when they are suspended on a concerted basis and suspend the provision of a monopoly service in the market for a supplier of public or private goods or services.

§5. Restriction of Competition

127. One of the typical restrictions of competition is the unjustified implementation of legal actions that result in access or permanence in the market of actual or potential competitors.

128. The government has an exception in this point because it has permitted the establishment of restrictions through a resolution of the Regulation Board for public interests reasons. This is especially when specific, concrete and meaningful benefits to the satisfaction of general interest are generated in the field or industry in which they are established. Efficiency shall be increased, and benefits in favor of consumers or users shall be generated, justifying their application.

129. In that sense, the law allows the establishment of restrictions on competition in the following cases:

(1) to develop a State monopoly in favor of public interest;
(2) to develop strategic sectors in accordance with the Constitution of the Republic;

(3) for the provision of public services in accordance with the Constitution of the Republic;
(4) for technological and industrial development of the local economy; and
(5) to implement initiatives of affirmative actions in favor of the popular and solidarity economy.

§6. Monopolization and Abuse of Dominance

130. A State Monopoly is accepted when it is developed for public interest reasons. One reason could be to improve the benefits of public services.

131. Article 9 of the Law states that "It shall be understood that abuse of market power occurs when one or more economic operators, on the basis of their market power, by any means, prevent, restrict, falsify or distort competition, or adversely affect economic efficiency or general welfare."

§7. Concentrations

132. Article 14 sets forth which acts are considered as control by economic operators:

(a) Merger between companies or economic operators.
(b) Transferring all of the goods or things of a merchant.
(c) Direct or indirect acquisition of property or any right to shares or equity or debt securities that give any right to be converted into shares or equity, or have any influence on the decisions of the person issuing them, when such acquisition grants the acquirer control of, or substantial influence over it.
(d) Interlocking common administration.
(e) Any other agreement or act transferring assets belonging to an economic operator or a person or economic group in a factual or legal fashion, or granting the control or decisive influence on the decisions of ordinary or extraordinary administration of an economic operator.

§8. Joint Ventures

133. The law makes no distinction between association, union or group of companies. Nor does it contain specific rules governing the operation of joint ventures. That is why a joint venture comes to be regulated as a business association.

134. Clusters are not punishable by law; unless they incur in conducts contrary to the law.

135. In the case of sanctions, the total turnover of the joint venture would be considered, taking into account the individual turnover of its members.

Chapter 5. Consequences of Violations and Enforcement Institutions

§1. Administrative Enforcement

I. The Antitrust Authorities

A. *Formation, Composition*

136. The Act in Article 36 creates a specialized control body to carry out the provisions contained in the Act. The Superintendency of Control of Market Power is a part of the Function of Transparency and Social Control, the fifth power of the State according to the Constitution, and it is comprised by intendancies, units, technical divisions, and advisory bodies. This administrative structure is formed according to the Statute by Processes published in October 2012.

137. The Superintendent is not only a control body but also a research and study center, which is accessible to the public in general, to fully understand the Competition Law that is handled in Ecuador. It is also empowered with the ability to enter into international agreements and conventions in regulatory or antitrust policies of economic competence, as well as coercive jurisdiction.

138. The Superintendent is the head of this control body, who has the exclusive power to create, modify or delete institutional processes, according to the technical reports prepared by the General Coordination of Planning and International Affairs. Likewise, the people in charge of each unit have a responsibility to improve their processes continuously.

139. The Superintendence of Control of Market Power officially started its operation in September 2012, so it has not yet completed all the activities contemplated in the Act.

140. It is important to mention that the Superintendence is a body that is a part of the fifth power mentioned above, so it is not under the direct orders of the central government, that is the Executive Function; however, the same Act provides for the creation of the Board of Regulation (Article 35), which may issue compulsory rules on the matters within its jurisdiction, and may not alter or innovate legal provisions.

141. It should be pointed out that from the files to be discussed, as well as from resolutions to be reached, the Superintendence will have the ability to establish criteria, not mandatory, for future similar cases, understanding that it is an administrative body and not a judicial body, as in some countries.

B. Investigating Powers

142. As part of its internal organization, there are three National Directorates in the control body, which are: Investigation of Abuse of Market Power; Research of Restrictive Agreements and Practices; and, Unfair Practices Research.

Each one of them has a National Director, intendent, and specialized analysts.

C. Adjudicating Powers (Ascertaining and Sanctioning)

143. The Commission of Resolution of First Instance in accordance with the Statute by Processes of the Superintendency must meet the following powers and responsibilities:

(a) to conduct the public hearing prior to the resolution of first instance;
(b) to impose sanctions in accordance with Articles 78 and 79 of the Act;
(c) to order corrective measures in accordance with the Act and the Regulation;
(d) to order, pursuant to section 76 of the Act, additional measures for breach of previously imposed corrective measures;
(e) to adopt preventive measures in accordance with the Act and the Regulation;
(f) to order, at the suggestion of the investigation body, or upon a party's request, suspension, modification or revocation of the preventive measures provided for under or supervening circumstances, or which could not be known at the time of issuing the resolution;
(g) to authorize, deny or make the authorization of an economic concentration operation under compliance with certain conditions;
(h) to order deconcentration measures, corrective actions or termination of control by an economic operator over one or more other operators when the need arises;
(i) to impose penalty payments, where appropriate, in accordance with Article 85 of the Act;
(j) to approve, amend, or reject the compromise proposal submitted by the investigated economic operator or operators; and
(k) further duties assigned by the Superintendent of Control of Market Power, and those established in current legislation.

D. Other Institutional Tasks (Consultancy to Parliament/Government)

144. The Board of Regulation is comprised of the highest authorities of the Ministries of Production, Economic Policy, Strategic Sectors and Social Development. It will be presided by the Coordinating Minister of Production, Employment and

Competitiveness (Article 45 of the Regulation). They all are members of the Executive Branch. This is given by the power that such State has to exercise rectory, planning, public policy and regulation in the scope of this Act (Article 35). This is a situation similar to the relationship between the Superintendency of Banks and the Banking Board.

145. The formation of this Board has generated debate as to the quality of the members. Many private sectors felt that members should not belong to the Executive Branch, but to the Participation and Social Control Function through public merit competition, and to be experts on competition.

146. The actual problem is that in the absence of regulations that must be issued by this legislative body, there are "vacuums" that cannot be supplemented by any other public institution. Therefore, the work of the Superintendent is currently limited to the phase of "sweeping" of information, for not being able to initiate its regulatory duty.

II. Government Direct Enforcement Activities

147. One of the most criticized points of the Act, since its drafting, was the content of current Article 28.

148. Originally, it was stated that the establishment of restrictions to competition by Executive Decree was to be admissible for reasons of public interest. Presently, the text states:

> It is permissible to establish restrictions on competition, by resolution reasoned by the Board of Regulation, for motives of public interest in any sector of the national economy in the following cases:
>
> 1.- For the development of a State monopoly in favor of public interest;
> 2.- For the development of strategic sectors in accordance with the Constitution of the Republic;
> 3.- For the provision of public services in accordance with the Constitution of the Republic;
> 4.- For technological and industrial development of the local economy; and,
> 5.- For the implementation of affirmative action initiatives in favor of the popular and solidarity economy.
>
> The establishment of restrictions on competition will proceed when generating specific benefits, tangible and meaningful, to the satisfaction of the general interest, in the field or industry in which they are established; when efficiency is increased, and benefits be generated in favor of consumers or users, to justify the application of restrictions.

149. By the Act granting this power to the Board of Regulation and not to the President, in practice, does not change anything because we have to keep in mind that the members of the Board of Regulation are representatives of the Executive.

150. The cases that can motivate the establishment of restrictions on competition may fall into excessive discretion as the parameters on which it is based do not have a fixed horizon. Assessing the point of satisfaction of general interest is the same as assessing the level of dissatisfaction of general interest; all will depend on the extent to which it is made.

151. For the sake of a supposed efficiency to generate benefits to consumers, it may fall in vindictiveness aimed at harming those operators who were not aligned with the current policies; at least that is the feeling this statutory provision causes in the private sector.

III. Other Administrative Agencies Applying Antitrust Rules

152. The Ecuadorian Intellectual Property Institute will apply the sanctions provided for in this Act when they know and decide on matters of unfair competition related to intellectual property.

153. The National Council for Pricing and Revision of Prices of Drugs for Human Use, entity attached to the Ministry of Health as a national health authority in relation to pricing, revision and control of prices of drugs of human use and consumption.

154. It is the duty of the Ministry of Agriculture and Livestock to establish and apply, in accordance with the law, the necessary mechanisms so that prices of pesticides and related products do not distort the costs of agricultural production. The Ministry will ensure that farmers, especially those with fewer resources, acquire pesticides at the most reasonable prices. Subject to the Constitution, the law, and this regulation, pesticides will be of free formulation, manufacture, import, marketing and distribution.

IV. Administrative Fines

155. The Superintendency of Control of Market Power, in its power to punish practices that go against free competition, may determine the sanctions that seek to stop said practices, by imposing fines according to the total turnover of the offending economic operator in the immediately preceding fiscal year to imposition.

156. Nevertheless, the criteria setting the norm on which to base the imposition of sanctions respond to the size and characteristics of the market affected by the conduct, the market share of the economic operator, the scope and duration—taking into account also the effect on the rights and legitimate interests of consumers and other economic operators, as well as the benefits obtained as a result of anticompetitive conduct.

157. The Act also includes the aggravating and mitigating actions that influence the decision to apply a specific sanction.

158. Among aggravating factors are: the repeated commission of offenses; the position of leader or instigator of the infringement; adoption of measures to enforce or ensure compliance with unlawful conduct; and the lack of cooperation or obstruction of the work of inspectors.

159. While mitigating factors are: the implementation of actions to stop the infringement; non-enforcement of the prohibited conduct; the conduct of actions tending to repair the damage; and, mainly active and effective collaboration with the Superintendency.

160. Sanctions may be:

- slight infringements with fines of up to 8%;
- serious infringements with fines of up to 10%; and
- very serious infringements with fines of up to 12%.

161. In the case of groups of operators, the turnover will be determined in consideration of the turnover of their members.

162. In situations that it is not possible to delimit the turnover, infringements under the Act will be punished as follows:

- slight infringements with a fine between 50–2,000 minimum wages.
- serious infringements with a fine between 2,001–40,000 minimum wages. and,
- very serious infringements with fines of more than 40,000 minimum wages.

163. This is even more critical because the range to be applied to impose the fine on the economic operator is at the Regulator's discretion.

164. Despite the above, if the Superintendency determines that the benefits obtained as a result of a conduct contrary to the provisions of the Act are superior to the threshold of 8%, 10% and 12% of the total turnover of the offender, or amounts provided the minimum wages, the offender will be punished with an amount identical to those benefits. The problem here would be then, in the event that the Regulator mistakenly determines such benefits, and the fine would be applied in relation to them, what would happen to the economic operator who cannot pay the amount of the fine, while remedies filed by the economic operator are being discussed, and taking into account that they have no suspensive effect?

165. The sanctions issue was profoundly debated by economic sectors of the country. These sectors perceive the amounts of fines as "excessive" and "disproportionate." Affecting the company's profit directly could lead to a financial and economic imbalance that is causing more of an inconvenience in daily life. Considering that the average market profit is 12% to 15%, the company would lose this benefit, and in some cases, the company would not generate profit, or in the best case, not within ranges, it should afford to pay the fine by acquiring a debt.

166. Also, economic operators who have not provided the required information, or have provided incomplete or incorrect information, will be punished by a fine of up to 500 minimum wages.

167. However, sanctions are not only for legal persons. As noted above, individuals may also be subject to sanctions. Hence when incurred in very serious infringements, it may impose a fine of up to 500 minimum wages to each of their legal representatives, or to persons being part of the governing bodies, who are involved in the agreement or decision, depending on the degree of intervention or participation of said representatives or officers in determining or implementing the practice or infringing conduct.

168. Nevertheless, those persons who, being part of the management bodies, did not attend the meetings or had voted against or saved their vote, are excluded from the sanction.

169. It should be mentioned that the Act contemplates the use of fines and periodic penalty payments. The latter is intended to: stop in prohibited conduct or which has been sanctioned; meet commitments or conditions adopted in the resolutions and ordered in a resolution, order or agreement, without forgetting the duty of cooperation with the Superintendence bodies; and compliance with the preventive and/or corrective measures.

170. These periodic penalty payments may be applied alongside penalties and will be up to 200 minimum wages per day, representing a greater burden for the economic operator to handle these expenses.

171. There remains the question on whether establishing penalties for economic operators will be based on the Principle of Proportionality, or will respond only to subjective criteria.

172. The Act is clear in identifying the subject offenders who commit acts or referred omissions. Whether it be individuals or moral persons, both are required to comply with legal provisions. Perhaps one of the most important aspects is the fact that individuals controlling economic operators may also be accused, thereby forcing in an indirect way, the proper management of the same to avoid penalties.

173. However, the purpose of the Act is not to leave unpunished the act or omission that contravened the provisions of this Act. This can be seen better in the case that a group of economic operators (consortium, association, business group, joint venture) were fined; this must be paid even with contributions from each economic operator individually.

174. In this case, leaving open the possibility that members of this group are excluded from the fine if they prove: i) that they have not implemented the infringing decision or recommendation; or, ii) that they ignored the existence of the infringing decision or recommendation; or, iii) they were actively distanced from the infringing decision or recommendation before initiating the investigation.

175. The law contemplates the possibility of a "Commitment to cease" in two cases: i) before receiving any subpoena of a proceedings having been initiated; and, ii) at any time of an initiated process, just before the decision issued by the settlement body of the Superintendence of Control of Market Power has been handed down.

176. This commitment may be filed individually or collectively; however, they shall be processed on an individual basis, since the Superintendency must consider the seriousness of the alleged infringement.

177. In this commitment, the alleged offender may offer a commitment related to the immediate or gradual cessation of the events under investigation, or modification of aspects related to them. This commitment may likewise remedy, if any, damages, losses or effects that have occurred are occurring, or may occur in the relevant market and in consumers, due to their anticompetitive practices.

178. For this, the law authorizes the Superintendency to suspend terms and deadlines of the procedure up to a term of one hundred and twenty days to reach a commitment, suspending other deadlines. The "Commitment to cease" may be approved by the Superintendency within forty-five business days, and if deemed appropriate, the Superintendency may request to be changed.

179. This figure was used by some companies using raw materials containing transgenic (genetically modified), and that according to the law, it should be reported on their products. The Superintendency accepted these "Commitments to cease" and companies changed that behavior, thus preventing an administrative process from being initiated against them.

180. The only fine imposed by the Superintendency went to a mobile phone operator. The amount of the fine was USD 170 million. However, the company appealed the fine in the Administrative Court and in turn, eliminated the behavior that had caused the fine. This caused the fine to be declared void.

V. Administrative Injunctions and Other Restrictive Orders

181. The Act in Article 62 grants the substantiation body, based on a suggestion by the investigative body or upon request of who has filed a complaint, the taking of measures, such as: ordering the cessation of the conduct; the imposition of conditions; suspension of the effects of legal acts related to prohibited conduct; the adoption of positive behaviors; and those it deems appropriate, intended to preserve the conditions of the affected competitor and to prevent damage that collusive practices might cause, as well as to ensure the effectiveness of the final decision. These measures may be issued before or at any stage of the investigation procedure.

182. Yet, these measures may not be about deprivation of liberty, the prohibition to leave the country, or detention. The Regulation to the Act in Article 74 mentions that: *adoption of preventive measures could be issued for the term it deems appropriate, taking as parameters and action limits the intensity, proportionality and needs of damage that is pretended to be avoided.*

183. Similarly, it is possible that prior to issuance of the decision by the Superintendence of Control of Market Power, both the economic operator and the inquired party, related party, or denounced party, may present a commitment proposal whereby they undertake to cease the conduct under investigation and to remedy, if applicable, damages, losses or effects occurred, occurring, or that may occur by their anticompetitive practices in the relevant market and in consumers.

184. But, to evaluate the request of commitment to cease, and in the exercise of discretionary power, the Superintendence will consider continuous compliance of the following conditions:

- That all or part of investigated economic operators makes an acknowledgment of all or some facts in the complaint or charges. This acknowledgment must be credible in the light of the evidence held by the main file, or that have been submitted by the parties as part of the approval procedure of commitment to cease.
- That investigated economic operators offer remedy actions for verifying the cessation of the alleged anticompetitive practice, and to ensure that they will not be repeat offenders.

185. Furthermore, additional measures may be offered as evidence for the purpose of amendment of offenders. Also, in case relevant market conditions are substantially altered, the economic operator who made a commitment under this chapter may request the review of the agreed commitment to the Superintendence of Control of Market Power.

186. In the scenario of non-compliance of the agreed commitment, the Superintendence will initiate the process of implementation and application of penalties provided by in the Act and, if suitable, will take such corrective actions as may be appropriate.

187. The first case in which preventive measures were adopted was related to telecommunications. The Superintendence of Control of Market Power issued a measure suspending exclusivity clauses of lease agreements for the installation of mobile phone masts. The aim was to improve the quality of service for all operators, to enhance interconnection conditions and, at the same time, to lower costs.

188. In this particular case, operators are still within the mandatory period to prove what the special cases are, where exclusivity conditions are technically unavoidable. The Regulator from the beginning of the process remained the criterion to judge on a case-by-case basis so that these exclusivity conditions are kept.

VI. Interim Measures

189. Preventive measures, such as: i) an order to cease and desist the illicit conduct; ii) the imposition of conditions; iii) the suspension of the effects of any legal act related to the banned conduct; iv) the adoption of positive conduct; and v) any such considering pertinent aiming to preserve the competitive conditions, to avoid the harm that may be caused by the illicit conducts, and to assure the effectiveness of the final Resolution.

190. Preventive measures cannot consist of imprisonment or ban on leaving the country.

191. Preventive measures must be adjusted to the intensity, proportionality, and necessity of the harm it is intended to avoid.

192. Corrective measures towards establishing the competitive process, prevent, impede, suspend, correct, or revert conduct that is contrary to the law, and avoid that such conduct be repeated.

193. The cessation of the antitrust practice, even under established conditions, or terms;

194. The performance of actions or the execution of contracts, towards regenerating the competitiveness, even under certain conditions or terms.

§2. Civil Enforcement

I. Competent Civil Courts

195. According to our legal framework, the competent courts in the case of impugnation of an administrative act are the Administrative Tribunals, not the civil ones. There is a specific Administrative Act that regulates the procedure for impugnation.

196. In order to hear civil actions, our legislation empowers the Civil and Commercial Judges, who are independent of the Administrative Courts.

197. Sanctions against offenders of the Competition Act does not preclude the right of individuals to sue for the corresponding damages, in accordance with the rules of ordinary law, and the imposition of sanctions under criminal law, in case of constituting a criminal offense.

198. Depending on the type of civil action to be filed, the deadline for the submission of a claim varies from three to five years. In criminal cases, offenses punishable with restriction of liberty sentences shall be prescribed for a maximum time of deprivation of liberty sentence provided for in the criminal offense plus 50%; and, for offenses with non-deprivation of liberty sentences, they shall be prescribed for a maximum duration of the sentence plus 50%.

199. Related cases are not known yet.

II. Sanctions

A. Nullity

200. The petition to annul can be invoked in the three years after the administrative act is issued.

B. Damages

201. The civil courts are the competent jurisdiction for resolving damage claims.

C. Interim Measures

202. N/A.

§3. Criminal Enforcement

I. Criminal Sanctions for Antitrust Violations

203. The Act does not set forth specific criminal offenses for committing any anticompetitive conduct. However, sanctions are indeed set forth for conducts related to the provision of fraudulent information, forging public documents, and wilful use.

II. Other Application of Criminal Law to Relevant Conducts

204. In the case of having committed forging of public documents, in trade or bank public deed, in writing, or in any other legal action, whether by false signatures; by imitation or alteration of letters or signatures; for inventing conventions, provisions, obligations or releases; or for having inserted out of time in the documents; for addition or alteration of the terms, statements, or facts that these documents were intended to receive or prove, it shall be punished with ordinary imprisonment from six to nine years. (Criminal Code, Article 339, Official Gazette Supplement 147 Jan. 22, 1971).

III. Role of Prosecutors

205. The General Prosecutor may initiate a preliminary investigation or preliminary inquiry process, as the case may be when there is a presumption of a legal offense.

IV. Competent Criminal Courts

206. We do not have special Courts in Ecuador to exclusively rule on competition matters or commercial crimes. They are the same ordinary criminal Courts which have jurisdiction to hear the various cases that arise.

Part II. The Application of the Prohibitions

Chapter 1. Restrictive Agreements

207. The Act is clear in stating that economic operators involved in a merger are required to comply with the prior notice procedure, irrespective of whether the merger is horizontal or vertical (Article 16).

§1. Horizontal Agreements

I. Cartels

208. The Act prohibits the existence of cartels and all forms of organizations seeking to restrict agreements or reach to concerted practices to affect the market.

209. We are not aware of the existence of cases of cartels as such to date.

A. *Price Fixing*

210. The scope extends to agreements that oblige fixing sale or purchase prices.

211. It is considered a serious offense. The fine can be up to 10% of turnover

212. There are no records of sanctions for this cause yet.

B. *Market/Cliental Location*

213. It is considered a serious offense. The fine can be up to 10% of turnover

214. There are no records of sanctions for this cause yet.

C. Production/Innovation Limitation

215. It is considered a serious offense. The fine can be up to 10% of turnover

216. There are no records of sanctions for this cause yet.

D. Group Boycott

217. It becomes an abuse of market power according to Article 11, number 15 “The boycott aimed to limit market access or the exercise of competition by other companies.”

218. It is considered a serious offense. The fine can be up to 10% of turnover.

219. There are no records of sanctions for this cause yet.

E. Collusion on Other Objects

220. Depending on the size and characteristics of the affected market, the damage caused by the conduct may be classified as serious damage or very serious damage. The fine will go up from 10% to 12% of the turnover.

221. There are no records of sanctions for this cause yet.

II. Information Exchange Practices

222. The violation of trade secrets is considered as an unfair practice in the following cases: (i) information is secret in the understanding that, as a body or in the precise configuration and composition of its elements, is not generally known or readily accessible to the members of the circles that normally deal with the kind of information in question, (ii) information has commercial value, actual or potential, because it is a secret, (iii) in given circumstances, the person who legally has the information under control and has taken reasonable steps to keep it a secret.

The following practices are especially considered as unfair:

(a) The disclosure or exploitation, without authorization of its holder, of secrets to which it legitimately had access, but with the duty of confidentiality, or illegitimately, as a result of any of the acts referred to in the following paragraph or in number 8 of this article.
(b) Acquisition of undisclosed information when it results, in particular, from:
 (1) industrial or commercial espionage;
 (2) the breach of a contractual or legal obligation;
 (3) breach of trust;

(4) provocation to commit any of the acts referred to in paragraphs 1), 2) and 3); and,
(5) acquisition by a third party who knew or should have known that the acquisition involved one of the acts referred to in paragraphs 1), 2), 3) and 4).

223. Likewise, it is considered a restrictive agreement when information is exchanged to fix on a concerted basis or to manipulate prices, interest rates, fees, discounts, or other business or commercial conditions (Article 11)
There are no records of sanctions for this cause yet.

III. Cooperation Agreements

224. In the case of agreements for research and development, specialization, standardization, union to production, to buy or sell, the Regulator would not have jurisdiction to intervene in the association, as long as it is not arranged any causal set forth in Article 14 on economic concentration.

§2. Vertical Agreements

I. Distribution

A. Exclusive Distributorship

225. It becomes an abuse of market power according to Article 9, number 11: "fixing, imposition, limitation or unjustified establishment of conditions for the purchase, sale and exclusive distribution of goods or services."

226. It is a serious offense with a penalty of 10% of the total turnover of the economic operator.

B. Exclusive Dealing

227. It becomes an abuse of market power according to Article 9, number 19: "Establishing, imposing or suggesting exclusive distribution or sale contracts, non-competence clauses or similar, that are unjustified."

228. It is a serious offense with a penalty of 10% of the total turnover of the economic operator.

C. Selective Distribution

229. An agreement to or to limit supply is a serious restriction of competition, also the unjustified establishment of conditions for the exclusive distribution of goods and services.

D. Franchising

230. Our Antitrust Act does not establish any regulations in relation to franchising.

II. Technology Licensing

A. Patent Licensing

231. The Fourth Amending provision of the Regulation and Control of Market Power Organic Act states that upon request of a party, it may be granted compulsory licenses when practices that have been declared by order of the Superintendency of Control of Market Power as contrary to competition, particularly when they constitute an abuse of market power by the patent holder.

B. Trademark Licensing

232. N/A.

C. Know-How and Trade Secret Licensing

233. It is considered as an unfair practice—the divulgation and exploitation, without the authorization of the owner, secrets to which they have gained legitimate access, but with reserve duty. It is also considered to be industrial espionage and breach of trust.

Chapter 2. Dominant Undertakings' Prohibited Practices

§1. Exploitative Practices

I. Excessive/Unfair Pricing

234. It is considered a serious offense. The fine can be up to 10% of the turnover. There are no records of sanctions for this cause yet.

II. Discrimination

235. It is considered a serious offense. The fine can be up to 10% of the turnover. There are no records of sanctions for this cause yet.

§2. Exclusionary Practices

I. Predation

236. It is considered a serious offense. The fine can be up to 10% of the turnover.

237. There are no records of sanctions for this cause yet.

II. Tying

238. It is considered a serious offense. The fine can be up to 10% of the turnover.

239. There are no records of sanctions for this cause yet.

III. Rebates

240. It is considered a serious offense. The fine can be up to 10% of the turnover.

241. There are no records of sanctions for this cause yet.

IV. Refusal to Deal

242. It is considered a serious offense. The fine can be up to 10% of the turnover.

243. There are no records of sanctions for this cause yet.

V. Price Squeeze

244. It is considered a serious offense. The fine can be up to 10% of the turnover.

245. There are no records of sanctions for this cause yet.

246. There are no records of sanctions for exploitative and exclusionary practices yet.

Chapter 3. Concentrations

247. The Antitrust Act does not establish a difference between horizontal and vertical mergers. If a merger fits in one of the following conditions, the merger notification is mandatory:

248. Total assets transference, acquisition, relationship trough common administration and for a legal transference, title and form; and a fact transference, use and enjoyment in the same person.

§1. Horizontal Mergers

249. The law considers as an abuse of market power to the behaviors of one or more economic operators with market power, under conditions where due to the concentration of the means of production or marketing, these behaviors affect or may affect, limit or prevent participation of their competitors or prejudice direct producers, consumers and/or users. (Article 9)

§2. Vertical Mergers

250. It is considered as a restrictive practice when the provision of a monopoly service in the market to a supplier of goods or public or private services is suspended on a concerted and vertical basis.

251. Similarly, it is considered as a restrictive agreement when the distribution or marketing of goods or services to deliver, restrict, limit, paralyze, establish obligations or control production is controlled on a concerted basis.

§3. Market/Product Extension Mergers

252. N/A.

§4. Pure Conglomerate Mergers

253. N/A.

§5. Joint Ventures

254. N/A.

Part III. Administrative Procedure

Chapter 1. Administrative Investigations Before the Antitrust Authority

§1. INITIATIVE

I. General Sectors Inquiries

255. The Antitrust Act sets forth the possibility for autonomous decentralized governments to receive complaints on competition issues, prior agreement with the Superintendency; however, as of this date, such agreements have not been signed. (Article 38 No. 16)

II. Ex Officio Investigations

Pre- Research Stage

256. The pre-research stage could be initiated ex officio, upon request from another government entity, following a complaint filed by the offended party or filed by any moral person or legal person who demonstrates having a legitimate interest.

III. Complaints

257. The complaint shall contain basic details of the complainant and the following information:

- identification of the alleged offenders;
- a detailed description of the reported conduct, stating the approximate period of its duration or imminence;
- the relationship of those involved with the reported conduct;
- identification data of involved individuals known by the complainant, including, among others, their addresses, telephone numbers and e-mails, involved, if any, if applicable, identification data of their legal representatives; lack of one or more requirements listed in this section does not invalidate the complaint;
- characteristics of the goods or services covered by the reported conduct, as well as the affected goods or services; and

– the evidence as it is reasonably available to the complainant.

258. The Body of substantiation shall verify that the complaint meets the legal requirements. In case the complaint is incomplete or unclear, the complainant shall be granted three days to fix it.

259. If the complaint is complete, such Body shall notify the alleged offender to submit its defense within a term of fifteen days.

260. If the complaint has not been modified within three days, its file shall be ordered without further procedure.

§2. Powers

I. Requests for Information

Sweeping

261. According to the provisions of Article 38, number 1 of the Act, it is one of the duties of the Superintendent of Market Power Control to conduct studies and market research that he considers relevant. To achieve this duty, the Superintendent may require from the individuals and public authorities some documentation and collaboration deemed as necessary, and according to the information gathered, and if appropriate, to initiate the investigation process.

Pre- Research Stage

262. The Superintendency may request information through public and private institutions. A peculiarity of this stage is that it is not necessary to give prior notice to the defendant or to the person to request information or documentation, once the file is opened.

263. The law also states that if the file of the complaint was ordered, and if there was enough motivation to do so, the offender shall have the right to sue in the courts for compensation for damages which would have been incurred.

II. Investigating and Search Powers

Pre- Research Stage

264. If the processing body were to have clear substantiation elements to allow it to have a reasonable doubt about the existence of an infringement, it would begin the next stage, by a reasoned decision.

Research Stage

265. This stage will last 180 days, renewable once for 180 days. Here the Superintendence is empowered to perform several proceedings in order to determine items of evidence such as: to take the testimony of persons under investigation, conduct inspections with or without notice.

266. After this stage, the proceeding body will order the notification of the complaint and indictment to the accused party, if any, so the accused party be able to reply to the same and file preliminary objections.

267. The basis for assessment may be applied, which are used to define markets, such as actual examples of substitution between two products, quantitative testing, customers' and competitors' opinions, consumer preferences. These criteria will help to define the market of the relevant product, properties and use, price, consumers' preferences, different categories of customers, barriers and costs that limit or prevent the effective replacement.

268. Once the corresponding proceedings are performed, a preliminary report will be drafted with the results of the investigation. If needed, the opening of the discovery period of sixty days will be ordered, renewable for another thirty days.

269. After the trial period, a final report will be submitted within a period of fifteen days. If the existence of infringement was determined, based on evidence, a report containing the offense, penalties and corrective measures will be issued.

III. Cooperation with Other State Institutions

270. One of the powers of the Superintendency is to coordinate the actions that were necessary and to execute cooperation agreements with public and private entities, in order to promote free competition of economic operators to different markets.

271. So far, the Superintendency has signed agreements with eight universities, three of them public universities, as well as with the following public entities: Intellectual Property Ecuadorian Institute; Judicial Council; Superintendency of Telecommunications; National Secretariat Telecommunications; National Secretariat of Higher Education, Science, Technology and Innovation; Ministry of Tourism; Central Bank.

272. As for international conventions, the Superintendency has signed agreements with the Federal Competition Authority of Austria; Ministry of Economy and Finance of the French Republic; Competition Defense of the Eastern Republic of Uruguay; the Hellenic Competition Commission; Ministry of Commerce and Craftsmanship of the Republic of Tunisia; Court of Defense for Free Competition of the Republic of Chile; Competition Authority of the French Republic; United Nations Conference on Trade and Development (UNCTAD), Competition National

Commission of Spain; National Economic Prosecutor of Chile; National Commission for Defense of Competition of the Argentine Republic; Federal Competition Commission of the United States of Mexico.

§3. RIGHT OF DEFENSE

I. Content and Notification of Opening Decisions

Resolution Stage

273. A Resolution Commission will hear the final report, and upon receipt of the file, the Commission will notify to the parties within three days.

II. The Proceedings: Hearings, Access to File, Briefs

Resolution Stage

274. From the notification, the parties have a ten-day term to file pleadings. Within this period, the parties may plead and file documents and evidence they deem relevant.

III. Statement of Objections

275. The law sets forth the Term for Exceptions (Article 58) which is given once the investigation is concluded, and if there is merit for continuing the process, the body of substantiation shall order so that the defendant be notified with the complaint and indictment. Once notified, the defendant, within a term of fifteen days, shall answer and set forth exceptions.

276. If the defendant does not reply to the complaint within the term provided, the process shall continue in absentia. During the process, the defendant shall have the right to access and request copies of all proceedings of the record.

IV. Final Hearing and Decision

Resolution Stage

277. If deemed necessary, both the processing body as well as the resolution body may call a public hearing. After this stage, the commission will issue a final reasoned decision. The commission will have ninety days to decide.

Chapter 2. Voluntary Notifications and Clearance Decisions

278. In cases in which concentration transactions do not meet any of the restrictive conditions, the authorization from the Superintendence of Control of Market Power should not be required.

279. Compulsory notifications.

Chapter 3. Merger Control

§1. Preliminary Filing Obligations

I. Criteria and Thresholds

280. There are two conditions under which the Act is based for the economic operator to be required to make prior notification of concentration (Article 16). One of the following conditions will suffice:

- That the total turnover in Ecuador of all participants exceeds, in the financial year preceding the operation, the amount that in current minimum wages, is set forth by the Board of Regulation.
- In the case of concentrations involving economic operators engaged in the same activity, and as a result of the concentration, a share equal or higher than 30% of the relevant market is acquired or increased for the product or service in a local field, or in a defined geographic market within the same.

281. In the first case and in the absence of legislation, this condition is not applicable in practice; therefore, required notices are currently made based on the second condition.

II. Turnover Calculation

282. For the purposes of this Act, the term total turnover of one or more economic operators, the amount resulting from the sale of products and provision of services performed by them during the last financial year corresponding to their ordinary after deduction of value-added tax and other taxes directly related to the final consumer with the business.

III. Market Share Calculation

283. *Also see the* relevant market.

284. The Superintendence uses the following indicators and procedures for conducting market analysis: Hefindahl-Hirschmann Index (HHI); Gini Coefficient; concentration of the four largest companies (C4); Measures of dominant position and competitiveness measures.

285. National Economic Census data are also used; the last time that a census was done was in 2010. The presentation of results follows the International Standard Industrial Classification of All Economic Activities (ISIC).

286. In the last issue of "Competition Sector Analysis" conducted by the Superintendency, from 1498 economic sectors disaggregated to ISIC 6-digit, and calculated from sales revenues, 64% of the economic sectors are highly concentrated; 11% are moderately concentrated; and, 25% are considered competitive.

287. However, using actual and referential HHI methodology, it was determined that there is a high capacity to distort the market in 34% of the sectors of the economy; 15% has a moderate distortion capacity; and, 51% has a limited capacity of distortion. Financial activities and cement manufacturers have the greatest market power as compared to food products, retail sectors and several other sectors which have the lowest percentage of market power.

288. Also, using the Gini coefficient, it was determined that 55% of the sectors have high inequality; 37% have a moderate inequality; and, 8% have low inequality. The supply sectors of insurance services other than life insurance are the most unequal. Sectors of poultry breeding, life insurance policies, disability and double indemnity insurance are the most unequal; while the industrial sector and the inorganic medical gases sector are the most equal.

289. By C4 Concentration Index, it was found that in 73% of the sectors, the four largest companies concentrate total revenue, with the manufacturing of cement; transportation, distribution and supply of gaseous fuels; and financial activities are the main controllers; while sectors of drugs, retail and food products, retail sectors and several others are the least concentrated.

290. Therefore, we could say that most of the economic sectors are highly concentrated in Ecuador, avoiding any proper market share; but, nevertheless, there may be a market distortion in a few cases.

IV. Other Relevant Notions

291. The following operations are exempted from mandatory notification:

- acquisitions of non-voting shares, or bonds, debentures or any security convertible into non-voting shares; and
- acquisitions of companies or liquidated economic operators, or those who have not registered any activity in the country in the last three years.

§2. Structure of Proceedings

I. Preliminary Assessment and Full Investigation

292. Concentration operations requiring prior authorization will be notified for previous review within eight days from the date of the conclusion of the agreement.

293. Notification will be in writing, accompanied by the related draft legal act, along with basic information of economic operators; their financial statements for the last fiscal year; their market share; and, other details identifying the intended transaction.

II. Time Framework

294. The whole administrative procedure can last at least six months to one year.

III. Right of Defense

295. This is explained in the administrative procedure.

§3. Clearance and Conditional Clearance

296. N/A.

I. Conditions and Undertakings

297. N/A.

A. Content

298. N/A.

B. Timing

299. N/A.

§4. Relations with Other Merger Control Authorities

I. Other Authorities Within the Local Jurisdiction

300. See Other Administrative Agencies applying antitrust rules

II. International Coordination

301. We have international Cooperation Agreements with: The Hellenic Competition Commission, the Ministry of Commerce of Túnez, the Tribunal of Defense of the Free Competition of Chile and the Economic General Attorney of Chile. The Antitrust Authority of France, UNCTAD, the Spanish National Competence Commission, National Competence Defense Commission of Argentina, and the Federal Competence Commission of Mexico.

Chapter 4. Challenging of the Administrative Decision

§1. Competent Courts

302. According to Article 173 of the Constitution of the Republic, administrative acts of any State authority may be challenged, both by administrative proceedings, as before the corresponding bodies of the Judicial Function.

303. With reference to issued acts, protective actions can be filed, provided it is not framed within the inadmissibility under Article 42 of the Jurisdictional Safeguards and Constitutional Control Organic Act, namely:

(1) When the facts do not show that there is a violation of constitutional rights.
(2) Where acts are withdrawn or extinguished, unless damages that can be repaired result from such acts.
(3) When the claim is only challenging the constitutionality or legality of the act or omission, not involving a violation of rights.
(4) When the administrative act may be challenged in Courts unless it is shown that the way be neither appropriate nor effective.
(5) When the plaintiff's claim be the statement of a right.
(6) When it is related to Court orders.
(7) When the act or omission emanates from the National Electoral Council and may be challenged before the Electoral Dispute Tribunal.

304. This appeal is not suspensive regarding the preventive and corrective measures in any case, except the suspension of financial penalty, provided a bond is issued for 50% of the value set by the competition authority, by an insurance policy or bank guarantee issued in favor of the corresponding Court (Article 69 of the Act).

§2. Time Limits

305. Any legal act issued by the Superintendence may be challenged in Court, before the Administrative Court, within a period not exceeding ninety days from the notice of appeal.

§3. Scope of Judicial Review

306. A serious drawback of Ecuador is the lack of specialized Courts in commercial matters. These are heard in the Civil Courts, which causes saturation of the judicial system, leading commercial issues not to be treated by experts, within a reasonable period.

307. This has been one of the reasons why the alternative disputes resolution, such as arbitration and mediation, has had enough demand in recent years, due to it is a faster and safer output, compared to the frowned judicial system, which despite recent reforms introduced by the Government, still leaves much to be desired.

308. Likewise, slowness in the procedures for obtaining permits, licenses or registration is a barrier generated by the State itself against free competition, as it prevents minor operators, not having plenty of operational capacity nor resources, to be neglected by those who are able to overcome the entire bureaucratic ordeal.

Selected Bibliography

As this is a fairly new matter in Ecuador; there are no Ecuadorian authors to review.

Selected Bibliography

www.ingramcontent.com/pod-product-compliance
Ingram Content Group UK Ltd.
Pitfield, Milton Keynes, MK11 3LW, UK
UKHW020151290926
15471UKWH00004B/816

9 789403 522753